TESLA

The Tesla emblem looks like a cross-section of an electric motor.

TESLA

ODYSSEYS

KRISSY EBERTH

CREATIVE EDUCATION · CREATIVE PAPERBACKS

Published by Creative Education and Creative Paperbacks
P.O. Box 227, Mankato, Minnesota 56002
Creative Education and Creative Paperbacks
are imprints of The Creative Company
www.thecreativecompany.us

Design by Graham Morgan
Art direction by Tom Morgan
Edited by Jill Kalz

Images by Alamy (Barry King), Dreamstime (Info634860), Flickr (The Car Spy), Getty (Jasper Juinen/Bloomberg, SUZANNE CORDEIRO/AFP), Pexels (Duren Williams, Jacob Moore, SpaceX), Toronto Exhibition, Unsplash (David von Diemar, Jenny Ueberberg, Jorgen Hendriksen, Milan Csizmadia, Roberto Nickson, Tommy van Kessel, Vlad Tchompalov), Wikimedia Commons (Debbie Rowe, Elfenbeinturm, Mack Male, Mariordo [Mario Roberto Durán Ortiz], Mariordo/NRMA New Cars, Nicki Dugan, Paul VanDerWerf, Pixabay, SpaceX, Steve Jurvetson)

Library of Congress Cataloging-in-Publication Data
Names: Eberth, Kristin, author.
Title: Tesla / by Krissy Eberth.
Description: Mankato, Minnesota : Creative Education and Creative Paperbacks, [2025] | Series: Odysseys in business | Includes bibliographical references and index. | Audience: Ages 12–15 | Audience: Grades 7–9 | Summary: "A business survey for young adults of the electric vehicle (EV) manufacturing giant Tesla, covering the global company's cars and technology, history, and key leaders, including Elon Musk. Includes sidebars, a glossary, and further resources"—Provided by publisher.
Identifiers: LCCN 2023046713 (print) | LCCN 2023046714 (ebook) | ISBN 9781640269200 (library binding) | ISBN 9781682774700 (paperback) | ISBN 9798889890881 (ebook)
Subjects: LCSH: Tesla Motors—Juvenile literature. | Automobile industry and trade—United States—Juvenile literature. | Electric automobiles—United States—Juvenile literature. | Tesla automobiles—Juvenile literature.
Classification: LCC HD9710.U54 E34 2025 (print) | LCC HD9710.U54 (ebook) | DDC 338.7/62922930973—dc23/eng/20231109
LC record available at https://lccn.loc.gov/2023046713
LC ebook record available at https://lccn.loc.gov/2023046714

Printed in China

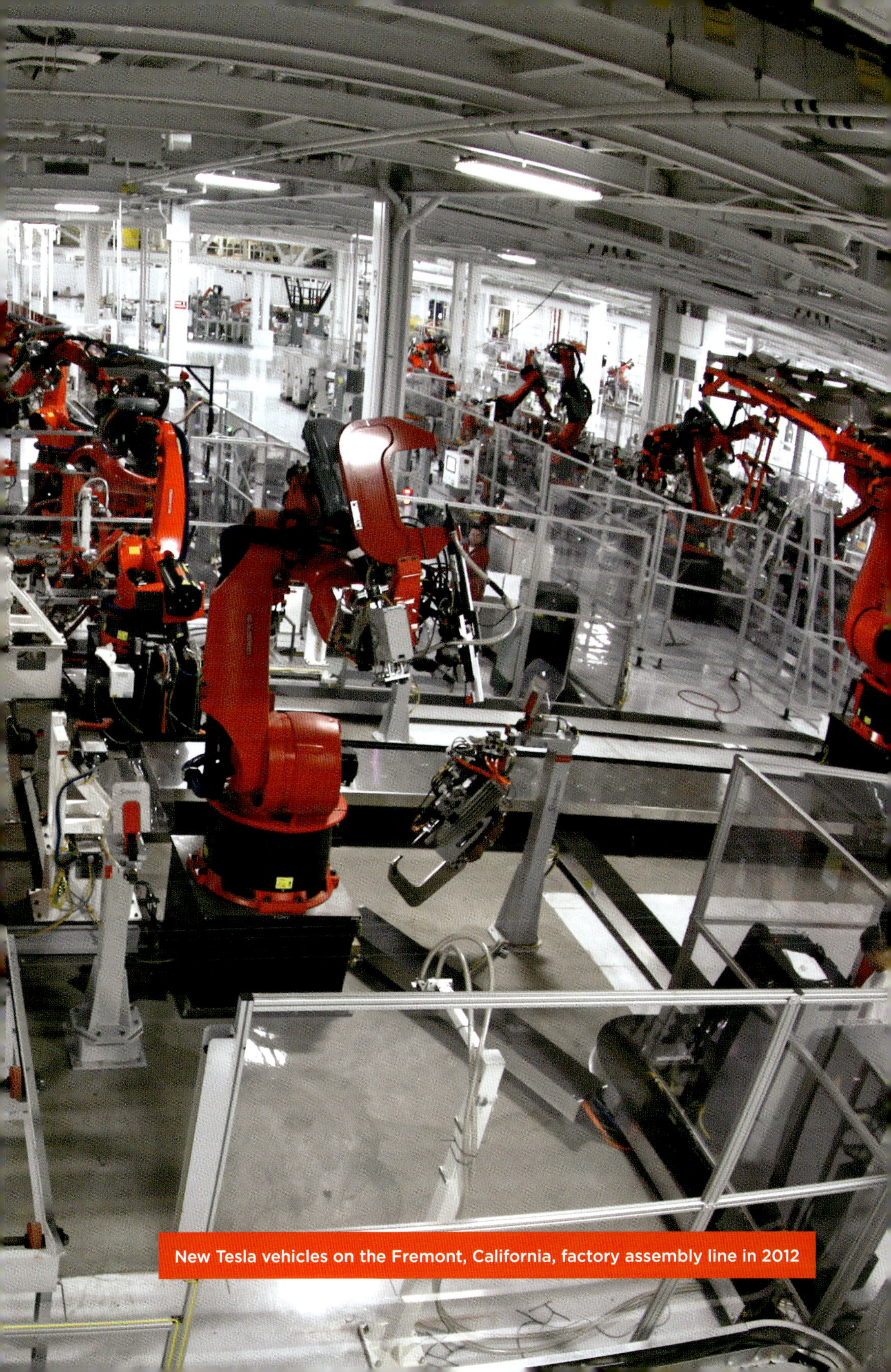

New Tesla vehicles on the Fremont, California, factory assembly line in 2012

Behind the wheel of a Tesla electric vehicle

CONTENTS

Introduction

Electric vehicles (EVs) are nothing new. Inventors have been working to make battery-powered vehicles since the mid-1800s. Even the wife of Henry Ford, founder of the Ford Motor Company, had an electric car. EVs were easier to start and drive than gas-powered vehicles.

OPPOSITE: Built in 1893, Canada's first electric vehicle, the Fetherstonhaugh, could go 15 miles (24 kilometers) per hour.

OPPOSITE Today's Tesla EVs are fast, fuel-efficient, and sporty.

But EVs were at a disadvantage. Gas-powered cars could go farther on a tank of gas than EVs on an electric charge. They were faster and cheaper. And at the time, the world's supply of fuel seemed bottomless. So, gas-powered cars became the norm.

Today, there are millions of cars around the globe. The majority burn gasoline and emit exhaust that's harmful to the environment. Gasoline is a fossil fuel and a finite natural resource. Burning it adds to global warming, the gradual increase in Earth's temperature due largely to high levels of **greenhouse gases** in the atmosphere. Growing interest in curbing global warming has led to increased interest in electric and **hybrid** vehicles. The challenge is to build an effective, efficient car that's better for the environment. Fun to drive would be nice, too.

One automaker has embraced that challenge. Enter, Tesla.

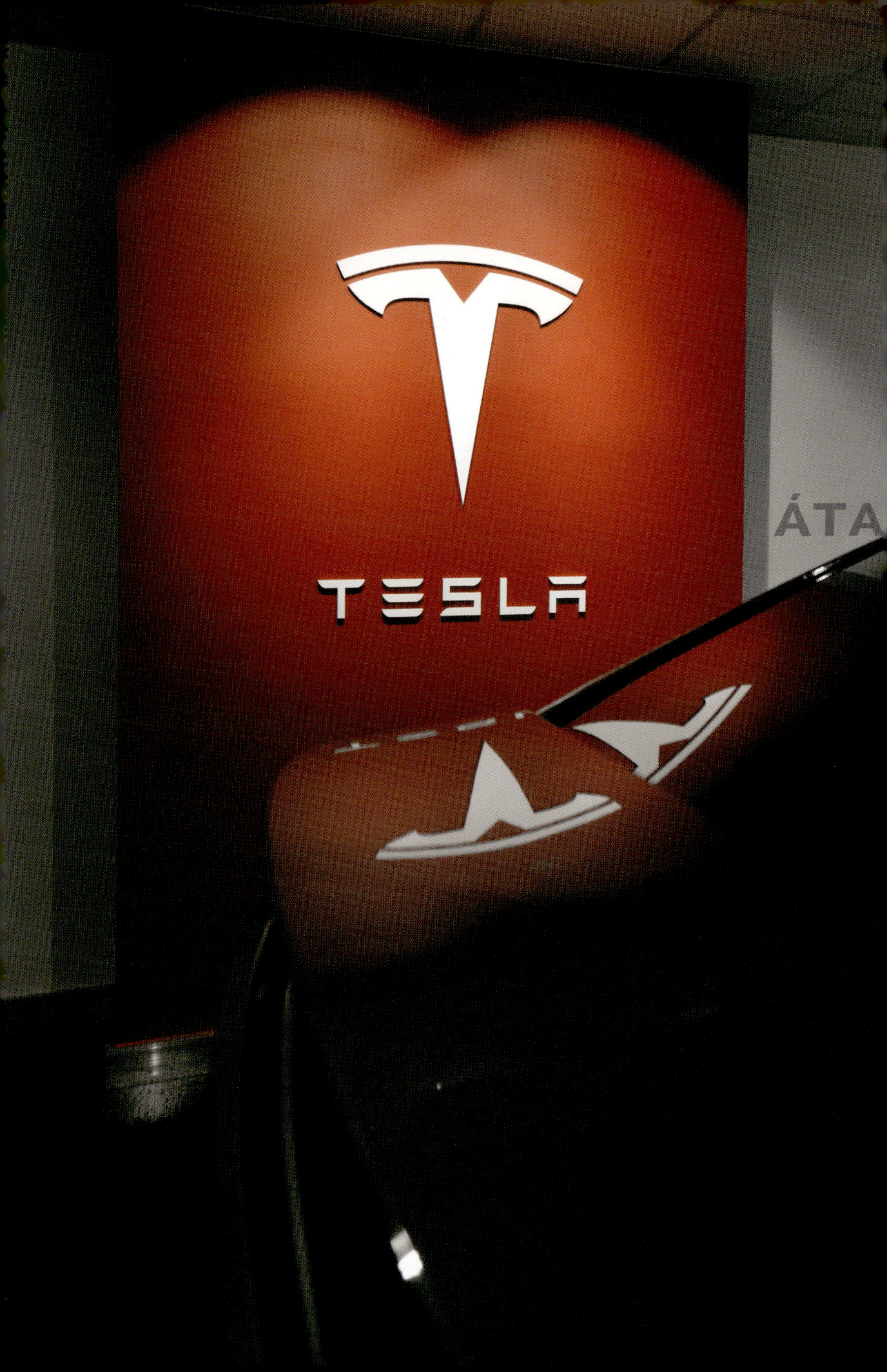
TESLA

Start Your Engine

Despite a short history, Tesla has become one of the most famous automakers in the world. It has changed the EV industry by creating and following what it calls its "master plan." What started as an interest in making a fast and fun electric car has led to new and exciting products and technology.

OPPOSITE: To many people, the Tesla name and emblem represent the best and most innovative EVs on the road today.

Tesla's ride so far has been wild. It's flirted with **bankruptcy**. But its goal has never wavered: to help the world combat climate change by creating products that use cleaner and more sustainable energy.

Tesla began its journey as Tesla Motors on July 1, 2003. It was founded by Martin Eberhard and Marc Tarpenning. They chose the name "Tesla" because it was catchy, it did not sound too "green," and it honored Nikola Tesla. Tesla was an engineer and inventor. He was awarded more than 300 patents for his **innovations** in power supply. He was also a pioneer of electricity and developed the first version of the AC electric motor that is used in some Tesla cars.

Eberhard and Tarpenning wanted to make EVs that were faster, more luxurious, and more fun than were currently available. They also wanted to create a combination of a car manufacturer and technology company that incorporated new battery and computer software technology. Eberhard was especially interested in lithium-ion batteries. These are the types of batteries typically used in laptop computers and other electronics. Eberhard became Tesla's chief **executive** officer (CEO), and Tarpenning became the chief financial officer (CFO).

Elon Musk joined Tesla in 2004 as an investor. Five years later, in a 2009 **lawsuit**, Eberhard sued Tesla and Musk for making false statements that damaged

Eberhard's reputation. He accused Musk of blaming him for some of the company's problems and of working to get rid of him. He also charged Musk with falsely claiming to be a founding partner of Tesla. Eventually, Eberhard dropped his lawsuit, and the dispute was settled. As a result of that lawsuit, however, Tesla is now said to have five cofounders: Eberhard, Tarpenning, Ian Wright, J. B. Straubel, and Musk. Each man brought an intense passion for computers and electronics to the table.

CEO Martin Eberhard grew up in California and then studied computer and mechanical engineering at the University of Illinois Urbana-Champaign. He loved sports cars and the environment. He founded a company called NuvoMedia with Marc Tarpenning in 1996. It created technology like today's Kindle e-reader. Eberhard

Tesla cofounder Martin Eberhard and the company's first product, the Roadster, in 2006

A Ford Model T

The First Electric Vehicles

The first electric vehicle was created in 1891 by William Morrison in Des Moines, Iowa. It was an electric wagon that held six passengers. Six years later, there were 12 electric cabs working in New York City. In 1898, Ferdinand Porsche created the P1, the world's first electric hybrid car. It was powered by both electricity and gasoline. By 1900, electric cars made up 30 percent of all vehicles in use. Once Henry Ford developed a way to mass produce his Model T car, the popularity of electric vehicles faded. The Model T cost less than half the price of an electric vehicle in 1912, making it more appealing to consumers.

and Tarpenning sold NuvoMedia in 2000 and were in the market for a new adventure. Three years later, Eberhard convinced Tarpenning to join him again in founding Tesla Motors.

CFO Marc Tarpenning also grew up in California and studied computer science at the University of California, Berkeley. He and Eberhard planned to utilize their computer and **entrepreneurial** expertise to develop electric sports cars. They knew nothing about building cars but felt that their curiosity would help them look at it from a unique perspective. Their goal was to produce electric cars that didn't compromise on mileage, handling, or luxury.

Ian Wright was originally from New Zealand and lived next door to Eberhard. He moved to the United States to build computer networking products. Eberhard had asked a start-up company named AC Propulsion to make him an electric car using lithium-ion batteries. He then asked Wright, an amateur race car driver, to test drive it for him. Wright was hooked. He quit his job, joined the team, and became Tesla's third employee.

TAKEAWAY

[Tarpenning and Eberhard] knew nothing about building cars but felt that their curiosity would help them look at it from a unique perspective.

J. B. Straubel grew up in Wisconsin and enjoyed rebuilding old electrical and mechanical gear he found at junkyards. He left Wisconsin for sunny California and studied engineering at Stanford University. While there, he became obsessed with developing an electric car. In his final year at Stanford, Straubel created an electric car and drag-raced every Saturday. His focus was

Tesla cofounder Elon Musk

the battery system, not the handling or mechanics. He joined Tesla in May 2004 as its chief technical officer.

Elon Musk grew up in South Africa. He moved to Canada when he was a teenager and studied at Queen's University. He later transferred to the University of Pennsylvania to study physics and economics. He planned to continue his education at Stanford but dropped out after only two days. He felt there was more opportunity in business and technology, so he went on to create a couple start-up companies, including PayPal. He sold

A SpaceX launch vehicle lifts off.

Not Just Tesla

Tesla is not the only company that Elon Musk runs or owns. He owns and operates SpaceX. SpaceX develops and launches reusable spacecraft, with a goal of someday sending people and cargo to Mars and other planets. Musk also owns the social media company X (formerly Twitter), The Boring Company, and Neuralink. The Boring Company digs tunnels with the goal of solving traffic problems within and between cities. Neuralink is a small start-up company that aims to connect the human brain to computers.

PayPal for $1.5 billion in 2002. In 2004, he invested $6.3 million in Tesla and became the chairman of the company's board of directors.

Musk was the driving force behind multiple rounds of additional funding. He helped Tesla raise more than $105 million from well-known people such as Google cofounders Larry Page and Sergey Brin. His popularity created buzz around Tesla. He was even the inspiration for Robert Downey Jr.'s portrayal of Tony Stark in the blockbuster movie *Iron Man* and its sequels. Musk wrote and posted "The Secret Tesla Motors Master Plan (Just Between You and Me)" on his blog in 2006.

The plan was simple:

- Step 1: Build a luxury electric sports car.
- Step 2: Build a luxury electric sedan.
- Step 3: Build an affordable electric car.

C007
TESLA

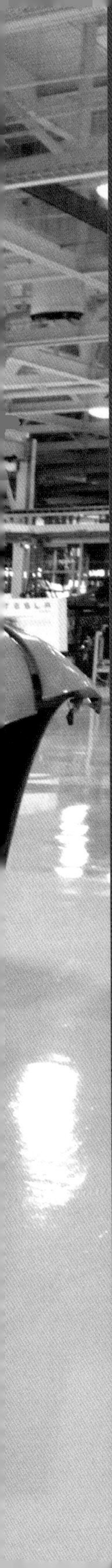

A Bumpy Road

The first step in Tesla's master plan called for the development of a luxury electric sports car. It was a tall order on its own—but an even bigger challenge for a team with hardly any experience in the auto industry. Companies with years of design experience had not been successful at making an EV. There were always problems.

OPPOSITE: Tesla factory tours are a perk offered to Tesla owners and any new buyers the owners might refer.

One problem with EVs is the battery. How do you create a battery system at an affordable price that produces enough power? The cost of the batteries adds thousands of dollars to the starting price of a car. Another problem for EVs is charging them. Where can customers charge their EV? Gas stations are everywhere. Charging stations are not. A third problem for EVs is their ability to work in cold weather. Batteries and cold temperatures don't usually mix. A fourth problem is that EVs might *not* be better for the environment. They require many special minerals that need to be mined, which often means destroying habitats or polluting soil, water, and air. And the final problem is that EVs generally do not make automakers any money.

Tesla was up for the challenge.

TAKEAWAY

EVs might *not* be better for the environment. They require many special minerals that need to be mined, which often means destroying habitats or polluting soil, water, and air.

In 2004, the company signed a contract with Lotus (a luxury car manufacturer) to work on the body of Tesla's first EV. It was called the Roadster. Originally, Tesla had planned to use more than 6,000 individual lithium-ion batteries to power each car. In tests, the batteries had provided the power to produce a car with quickness that stunned a group of engineers. Tesla was in the final stages of producing a lithium-ion battery pack when the battery industry realized how dangerous lithium-ion batteries

First-generation Roadsters came in colors such as Very Orange, Radiant Red, and Electric Blue.

22
23
AU58 JBE
GB

could be. When handled improperly, these types of batteries can overheat and catch fire. In fact, Apple Inc. and other electronics companies were recalling devices with lithium-ion batteries because of the danger.

Tesla's battery supplier tried to recall all the batteries it had sold to Tesla. Martin Eberhard decided to ignore the recall and moved forward with research into the problem. His engineers produced a plan to put a small amount of sludge-like liquid in between each of the batteries. The liquid kept the batteries from reaching a high enough temperature to set their cells on fire. This system contained the heat and prevented the batteries from overheating. Tesla had its answer to the battery problem and could continue working.

On July 19, 2006, Tesla held a huge party in Santa Monica, California, to unveil the **prototype** for the Roadster. It would be Tesla's first product, so the unveiling was important. Celebrities rubbed shoulders with politicians and tech industry leaders to get a look at the luxury electric sports car. By the end of the night, celebrities such as George Clooney had made down payments of $100,000 to order one of the first Roadsters produced.

The Roadster had a top speed of 125 miles (201 km) per hour. It was sleek, with a rich interior, and could go from 0 to 60 miles (97 km) per hour in under 4 seconds. These numbers made it comparable to gasoline-powered cars. Also, its lightweight body, made from carbon fiber, allowed the Roadster to travel 245 miles (394 km) on a single charge. This type of range had never been seen in EVs prior to the Roadster. It was thanks to the amazing engineering of the lithium-ion cell batteries.

Despite the Roadster's successful debut, however, things weren't all roses for Tesla behind the scenes. The management team was not getting along or working well together. In 2007, Eberhard was asked by the board of directors to step down as CEO. He did, but he continued to play a part in Tesla's future by participating on the company's advisory board. Eventually, however, in 2008, he cut all ties with Tesla. Marc Tarpenning, who was serving as CFO, also left the company.

Tesla had two more CEOs in a short amount of time. Michael Marks took over as CEO after Eberhard left but stepped down just a few months later. Ze'ev Drori was named the CEO in November 2007. He was credited with getting the Roadster out of the prototype phase and on the market. The first Roadster

For the Dogs

Tesla cars include Dog Mode. This unique feature is a climate control setting that allows people to leave their dogs in the car no matter what the temperature is outside. A screen shows passers-by a message that reads, "My owner will be back soon. Don't worry!" The message also includes the inside-car temperature. If the vehicle owner is gone for a long time, and their car's battery gets below 20 percent, a notification is sent to their phone to alert them of the situation.

was delivered to Elon Musk in February 2008. Tesla had successfully completed the first step of its master plan: develop a luxury electric sports car.

In October 2008, Musk replaced Drori as CEO. The entire world was having a financial crisis, and Musk had his work cut out for him. His priority was to get Tesla's cash flow going in a positive direction. The company needed to increase production and improve its **profit** margins while reducing expenses. Within a month of Musk taking over, Tesla eliminated about 25 percent of the company's staff. On top of that, Eberhard and Tarpenning soon filed a lawsuit against Musk. They accused him of forcing them out of the company that they had created. They lost their lawsuit, but it almost ruined Tesla.

Even though Tesla had successfully rolled out the Roadster, it was in major financial trouble. The company had very little cash to pay its bills. Without more cash, it would not be able to produce all the cars that had been ordered. Tesla was close to bankruptcy.

Daimler (a large car company) sent a group of engineers to Tesla to consider investing in it. The engineers were unreceptive at first. But once they rode in the Tesla car, they changed their minds about the little start-up company. The car was cool, fun, and handled like a dream. On April 20, 2010, Daimler purchased a 10 percent stake in the company for $50 million. This gave Tesla some breathing room and the ability to stay in business. After that, the U.S. Department of Energy provided a $465 million loan. Tesla was able to repay all of its loans, plus $12 million in interest. No other car company has been able to do this.

With its finances taken care of, Tesla moved its offices to Palo Alto, California, and continued to work its master plan. The next step was to develop a luxury electric sedan.

When a privately held company seeks to raise money for business expansion, it may decide to "go public." The company sells its **shares** to the public on the stock market. Tesla went public on June 29, 2010. Shares started at a price of $17 each, with the stock price of $1.59. The company raised $226 million in its **initial public offering** and was the first automaker in the United States to go public since Ford in 1956. Once shares finished trading, Tesla was valued at $2.22 billion. Musk and his team were beyond-the-moon excited.

Hold On to Your Hat

Tesla had figured out how to use lithium-ion batteries to power its $100,000 electric sports car, but it did not have an answer yet on how to charge them. Originally, the Roadster took 24 to 48 hours to fully charge. By comparison, it takes only minutes to fill a gas tank. After much research and development, Tesla engineers came up with "Supercharger" technology.

OPPOSITE: A Tesla Supercharger station delivers electricity to a vehicle's charging port through a cable.

Tesla charging stations are now available in all 50 U.S. states.

The chargers plug into the car in the same way as before but can power a car in under one hour—still longer than filling a gas tank but overall, an improvement.

Tesla dashboards provide drivers with a "range estimate." This gauge shows how many miles are left before the charge runs out. In the United States, the average driver commutes 37 miles (60 km) per day. Many EV drivers worried about making it to work or back home, especially if they had forgotten to charge their vehicle. Cold weather, too, could reduce a battery's remaining range and leave drivers stuck. In the early 2000s, gas stations were everywhere, but charging stations were few and far between. Many EV owners used the term "range anxiety" to describe their fear of being stranded. What Tesla needed was a network of charging stations that could eliminate all range anxiety.

On September 24, 2012, Tesla announced that it had secretly developed a Supercharger network. There were six stations in California, with more planned throughout the United States in 2012 and Europe and Asia in 2013. Musk himself announced the Supercharger network at a party. At first, nobody reacted to the announcement. Musk then explained that all Supercharger stations would have solar panels installed to provide the power. Again, nobody cared or realized what he was sharing. Finally, Musk said, "You'll be able to travel for free, forever, on pure sunlight!" That statement got people's attention.

As of April 2023, Tesla had more than 45,000 Supercharger stations around the world as part of its charging network. It is still working on creating charging stations that produce enough power through

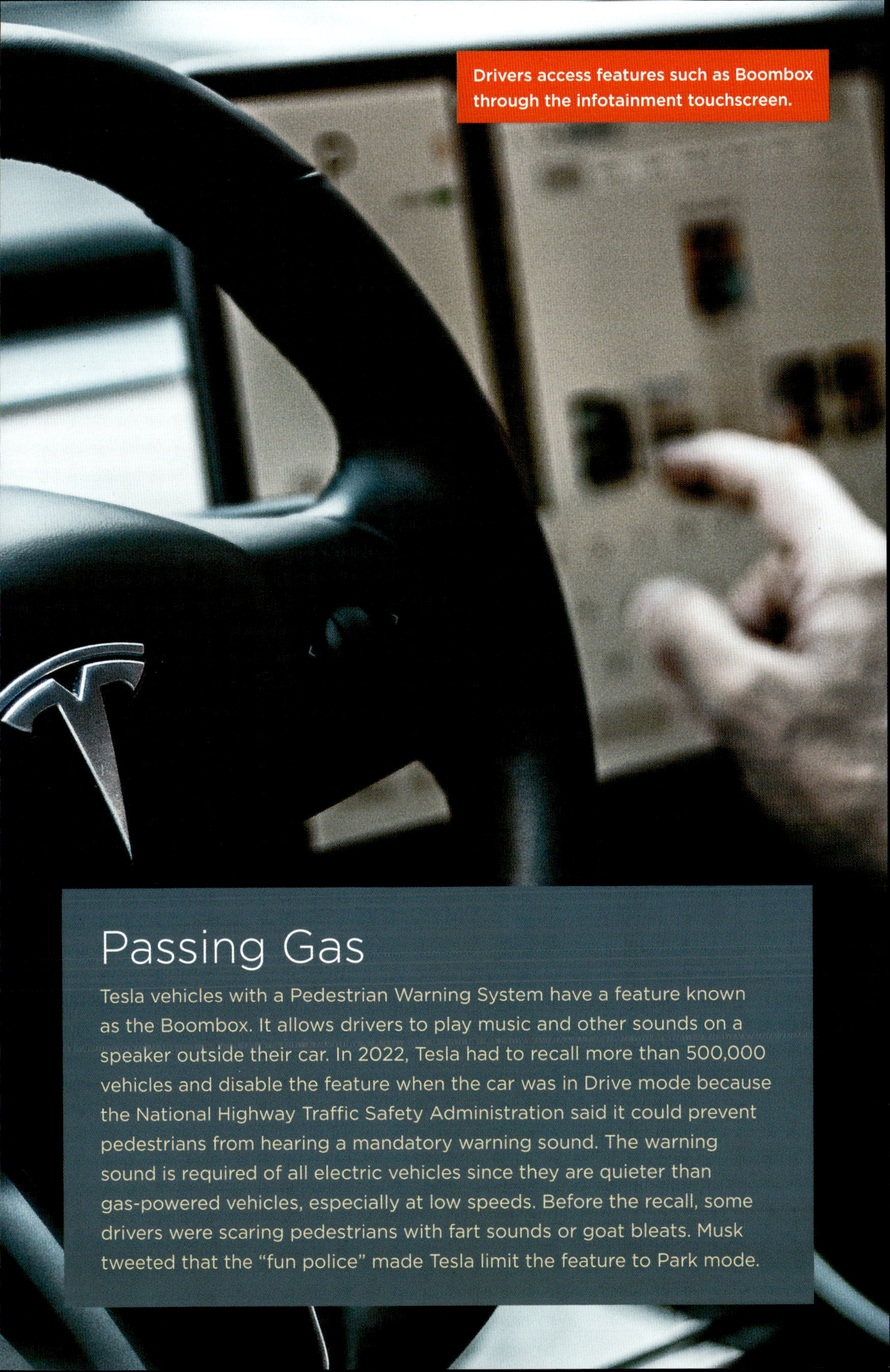

Drivers access features such as Boombox through the infotainment touchscreen.

Passing Gas

Tesla vehicles with a Pedestrian Warning System have a feature known as the Boombox. It allows drivers to play music and other sounds on a speaker outside their car. In 2022, Tesla had to recall more than 500,000 vehicles and disable the feature when the car was in Drive mode because the National Highway Traffic Safety Administration said it could prevent pedestrians from hearing a mandatory warning sound. The warning sound is required of all electric vehicles since they are quieter than gas-powered vehicles, especially at low speeds. Before the recall, some drivers were scaring pedestrians with fart sounds or goat bleats. Musk tweeted that the "fun police" made Tesla limit the feature to Park mode.

Tesla Model S

their own solar panels to enable Tesla customers to "drive for free on pure sunlight."

With the Supercharger network underway, the next step in Tesla's master plan was to develop a luxury electric sedan. The Model S was a huge success. Critics loved it. The high-performance battery allowed the Model S to go from 0 to 60 miles (97 km) per hour in 2.28 seconds. Tesla redesigned the interior by putting the battery system under the floor of the car, freeing up space in the back. This move also gave the car a lower center of gravity, which improved its handling. The Model S featured a range of 402 miles (647 km) per charge. It was sleek and stylish. In 2015 and 2016, the Model S was the bestselling EV in the world. It cost about $75,000 and went into full production in 2012. In 2013, Tesla made its first quarterly profit—10 years after its journey began. The stock price rose to $3.72.

Tesla on Autopilot

In 2014, Tesla unveiled "Tesla Autopilot." This technology uses **artificial intelligence**, with cameras and sensors to help the driver with braking, steering, and acceleration. It wasn't available for customers to purchase until 2015. In 2016, Musk claimed that Autopilot was "probably better" than a human driver. He promised that within two to three years, the technology would surpass human performance. He also announced that owners would be able to "summon" their Tesla to come to them from across the country.

Tragically, later that year, a man died in a crash while using Autopilot in his Model S. Tesla updated its Autopilot technology to make it safer—but not safe enough. Since then, more than 12 people have died in car crashes while Autopilot was in use. The National Highway Traffic Safety Administration has ongoing investigations about Autopilot's safety. Tesla, meanwhile, has continued to refine its technology.

In 2014, Tesla had set a goal of producing more than 500,000 cars per year. This required the company to figure out a way to get more lithium-ion batteries. Tesla needed to think big—GIGA big. Its solution was to build a factory that would produce batteries solely for Tesla and bring most of its manufacturing under one roof for maximum efficiency. Located in Nevada and called Gigafactory, the factory is one of the largest building footprints in the world. Tesla has also built Gigafactories

The prototype for Tesla's Model X was unveiled in 2012.

in Buffalo, New York; Reno, Nevada; Shanghai, China; Berlin, Germany; and Austin, Texas.

Tesla decided to get into the popular "crossover" market in 2015 with the Model X. The midsize crossover upped the cool factor, featuring "falcon-wing" rear doors that opened straight up. In 2016, the company jumped into another hot market: energy. It acquired Solar City and utilized Solar City's technology to manufacture solar panels, EV chargers, and solar batteries. Tesla then produced the Powerwall, Powerpack, and Solar Roof. These energy products utilized Tesla's battery technology. The Powerwall is a lithium-ion battery pack designed to power an entire home. The Powerpack is similar but is used to power a small business or project. The Solar Roof turns a normal roof into an energy-producing one.

After the purchase of Solar City, Musk announced that Tesla would add four goals to its master plan. First, it would develop rooftop solar panels with its new subsidiary, "Tesla Energy." Second, it would develop more affordable vehicles. Third, it would improve Autopilot's technology to a level "10 times

All doors on the Tesla Model X, including the falcon-wing rear doors, are electrically powered.

The headlight of a Tesla Model 3

safer" than human performance. And lastly, it would create a car-sharing program.

Tesla's Model 3 started production in 2017. It had a hefty battery range of 353 miles (568 km) and a roof made entirely of glass. Its price tag was $35,000. The cheaper price point made owning a Tesla attainable to the mass market. There were almost 500,000 orders within a year. This marked a big transition for Tesla—changing from a small company making luxury cars to a full-fledged automaker making cars for the public. Musk boasted

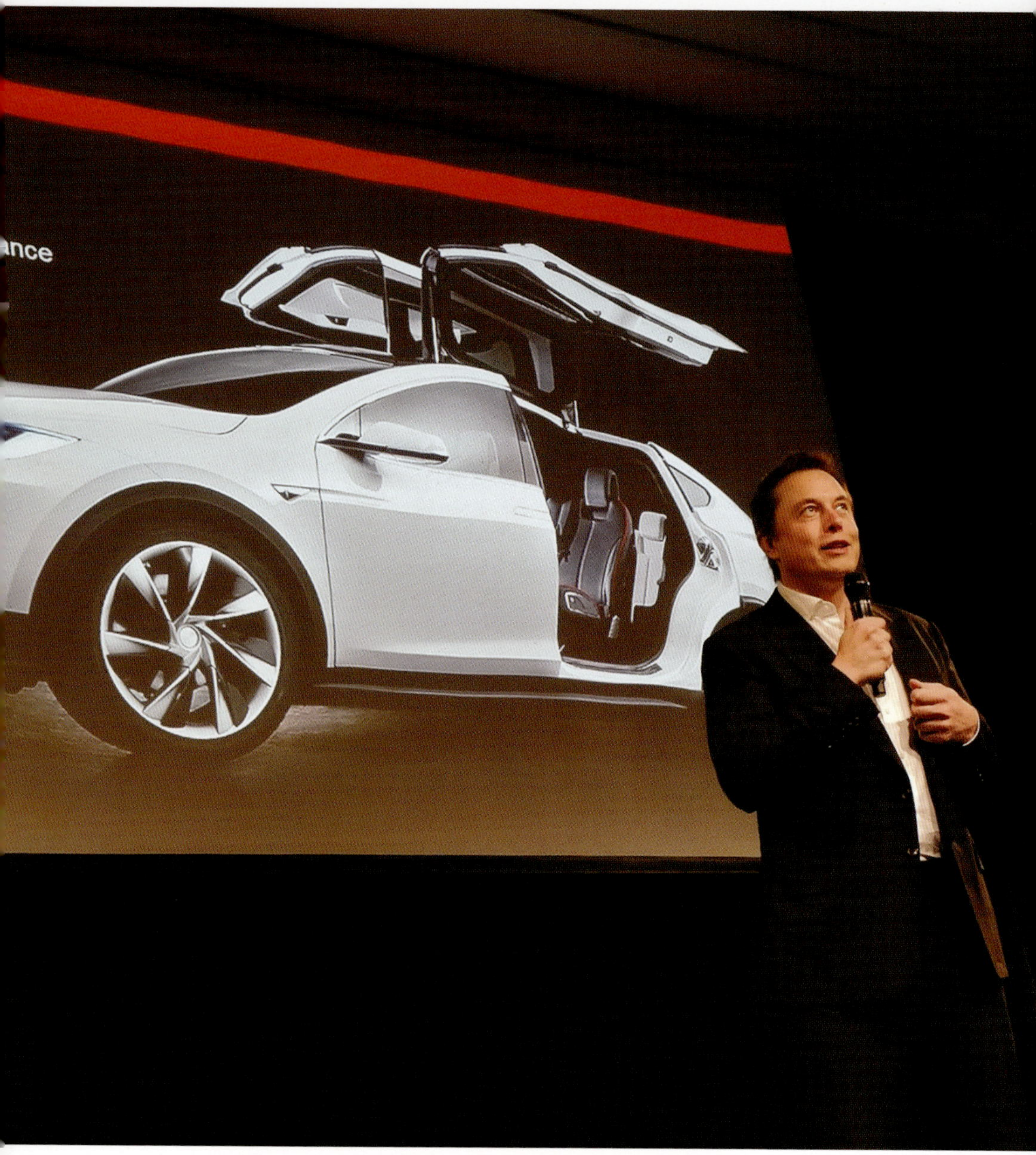

Elon Musk shared info about the 2015 Tesla Model X at the 2014 annual shareholders' meeting.

that Tesla could produce up to 200,000 vehicles in the final six months of 2017. This claim would equal a huge, almost quadruple, increase in productivity. Tesla could not produce the promised cars. In fact, it ran into trouble trying to manufacture the Model 3. This was not the first time Musk had made a bold statement the company couldn't back up. And it wouldn't be the last.

Tesla ran into more trouble in 2018. It continued to have issues producing enough cars. It missed its earnings predictions. The news scared investors, and they started selling Tesla stock. The company lost a lot of its value. Frustrated, Musk tweeted that he would reverse the company's standing and make it private again. This announcement suggested a positive change for Tesla and made investors want to buy shares again. The stock price went up.

Shortly after, lawsuits were filed against Tesla. The Securities and Exchange Commission (SEC) started an investigation into Tesla for **fraud**. Musk was accused of making false statements for the sole purpose of making Tesla's

Keep On Truckin'

Tesla announced plans to develop a fully electric semitruck in 2017. Five years later, the Tesla Semi debuted. The first orders went to PepsiCo. Tesla claims the Semi can pull three times the amount that a traditional diesel semitruck can. It also claims the Semi can save companies up to $200,000 in fuel costs within its first three years of operation. Styled in a futuristic way, the Semi has the driver sitting in the center of the cab instead of off to the side. The truck's battery can go 500 miles (805 km) on a charge and can be recharged within 30 to 90 minutes.

As of 2023, more than 230 company-owned Tesla showrooms were operating in the United States.

stock rise. He ended up paying a fine of $20 million. His Twitter account and all communications were subjected to mandatory review by an independent committee of directors. Musk was replaced by Robyn Denholm on the board of directors for Tesla, although he retained his position as CEO. In addition to Musk, Tesla was fined $20 million by the SEC, too.

In March 2019, Tesla announced its Model Y. It was the last step in the company's original master plan. The Model Y is a smaller, more affordable electric vehicle. It is similar to the Model 3, with its sleek styling and luxurious interior. It has three rows of seats, ample cargo space, and a battery range of 326 miles (525 km). Musk expected the Model Y to become Tesla's best-selling model and to help grow the company's value. Time would tell.

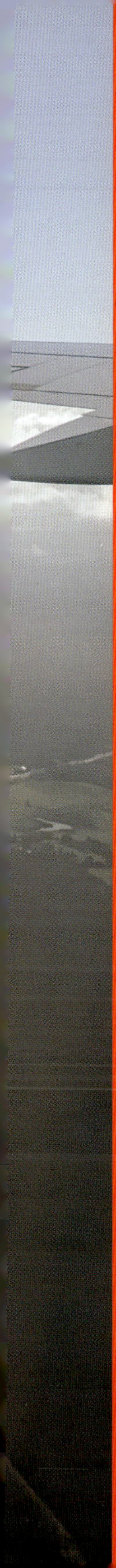

Onward and Upward

EVs are often touted as being better for the environment than gas-powered vehicles. While they don't burn gasoline and release exhaust, that doesn't automatically mean they are better. One way to measure an object's impact on the environment is by looking at its **carbon footprint**. For Tesla, the carbon footprint of its vehicles relies on three major factors.

OPPOSITE: Tesla's Gigafactory Berlin-Brandenburg employs about 11,000 people who produce mostly Model Ys and batteries.

The first factor is Tesla's Gigafactories. At this point, Tesla is just starting to disclose information about factory emissions, so it's unclear what effect the gases are having on the environment. Other car manufacturers are much more open about the gases they release.

Tesla's carbon footprint is also tied to how the electricity is produced that powers its cars. Many areas of the world still use older technology to power charging stations, technology that has a larger carbon footprint. However, a growing number of areas are using greener energy sources such as wind and solar. Green energy has a much smaller carbon footprint.

Lastly, even though Tesla's EVs run cleaner, their specialized lithium-ion battery packs have a large carbon footprint. According to a study by Argonne National Lab, it takes about three years of average driving to offset the carbon footprint of Tesla's battery pack. Tesla vehicles also require specialized metals that are mined throughout the world. Although mining isn't a huge contributor to carbon emissions, Tesla has vowed to work closely with mines to create as small a carbon footprint as possible.

Confidence in Tesla's ability to maximize EV efficiency while minimizing the impact on the environment has wavered a bit through the years. But the company has always trended upward. Tesla's stock price steadily grew from 2010 to 2013. In 2010, its stock was priced at $1.59. By 2013, it was $3.72. Later that year, the announcement of the Autopilot boosted Tesla's stock price to $10.01. The company's expansion into the energy industry and development of Gigafactories drove the stock up to $13.99. Once it started delivering its vehicles, the stock rose substantially. The delivery of the first Model 3s pushed Tesla's stock to $22.34. The stock declined slightly as Tesla missed some production targets but rebounded in late 2018, to $25.30, when Musk made some tweets. After the SEC tangled with Musk, the stock price fell again to $19.26. Delivery of the Model Y was a turning point. Tesla stock shot to $49.57.

Even through the COVID-19 pandemic, Tesla's stock price rose. Tesla had announced the production of the Model 3 in China in March 2020, just as the pandemic was starting. Musk tweeted, "The coronavirus

Tesla factories use as much automation as possible to build vehicles.

A Money Yo-Yo

Who is the richest person in the world? Elon Musk went from a net worth of $25 billion in 2020 to $266 billion in 2021. This made him the richest private citizen in the world. His wealth is tied directly to Tesla's stock value. He also holds the Guinness World Record as the person who has lost the most money ever. Musk's peak net worth was $340 billion in November of 2021. After that, he lost about $200 million, when Tesla's stock price dropped. He has gone back and forth as the richest person in the world, depending on how Tesla does financially. In 2023, he was back at the top spot.

is dumb." Initially, he worried the pandemic would hurt Tesla's momentum. But as countless companies shut their doors, and the world watched the health crisis unfold, Tesla grew. The Chinese government allowed the Tesla factory to continue producing cars at the start of the pandemic. They even helped coordinate housing, masks, and sanitizer for the thousands of factory workers.

Ultimately, Tesla did close, like so many other manufacturers around the world. But it handled the economic instability of the pandemic better than most. In June 2020, Tesla stock was at $66.06, and only a month later, the price hit $106.16. Tesla had four quarters of profit under its belt, and its stock price in August was $166.11. By December, the stock price was $216.62. Tesla saw ridiculous growth in the year 2020, with its share price increasing 740 percent from start to finish.

Less than a year later, in October 2021, its valuation reached $1 trillion.

Tesla is always looking toward the future. In 2021, it saw Bitcoin as an opportunity. The digital currency is a way for people to send money over the Internet. It operates with no supervision from banks or governments, and its value goes up and down. Tesla invested more than $1.5 billion in Bitcoin and allowed customers to pay for their vehicles using it. This move created interest in the currency. More people started investing in it, which made its value rise.

TAKEAWAY

Tesla saw ridiculous growth in the year 2020, with its share price increasing 740 percent from start to finish. Less than a year later, in October 2021, its valuation reached $1 trillion.

Tesla quickly earned more than $100 million from its Bitcoin investments. But after a few months, the company stopped allowing customers to use Bitcoin as payment for their vehicles. It stated that it was concerned about how Bitcoin contributed to the use of fossil fuels. After that,

Musk addressed guests at a party to celebrate a new Tesla factory in Austin, Texas, in 2022.

Bitcoin's value declined, and in 2022, Tesla sold more than 75 percent of its Bitcoin holdings. In all, Tesla lost more than $200 million from the currency investment.

In December 2021, Tesla moved its headquarters to Austin, Texas. It continued to see strong vehicle sales in 2022, bringing in $67.2 billion—a 51 percent jump over 2021. The increase was mostly due to Model Y production. In addition to vehicle sales, Tesla's **revenue** comes from services, energy generation and storage, vehicle leasing, and automotive regulatory credits. In 2023, the Society for Automotive Engineers announced plans to use Tesla's technology for plugging in EVs. Tesla calls this technology the "North American Charging Standard." The unique plug and system were created by Tesla and have been used in their vehicles since 2012. General Motors, Ford, Mercedes-Benz, Polestar, Rivian, and Volvo plan to use this charging system in their EVs.

Tesla and its CEO, Elon Musk, have weathered lots of criticism and controversy in their short history together—from Musk's bold announcements and tweets to SEC violations and fines, from near bankruptcy to a $1 trillion valuation. Through it all, Tesla has created an amazing company like no other, with an array of innovations. It has launched itself into new markets in big ways and worked to make clean energy and clean transportation attainable for all.

Space Highway

On February 6, 2018, SpaceX launched the Falcon Heavy. The reusable space rocket was designed to carry cargo into Earth's orbit. The cargo on this flight was Elon Musk's midnight cherry Roadster, with Starman (a test mannequin) at the wheel. During the launch, Starman listened to the song "Space Oddity," by David Bowie, on loop. The launch was live-streamed on YouTube to 2.3 million viewers. As of January 2024, the Roadster was still orbiting Earth. It had gone around the sun more than 3.8 times since launch.

Selected Bibliography

Dean, Grace. "Tesla Revenue Isn't All from EV Sales. Here's Where Its Billions of Dollars a Year Come From." *Insider.* July 3, 2023. https://www.businessinsider.com/tesla-revenue.

EPA. "Electric Vehicle Myths." Accessed August 29, 2023. https://www.epa.gov/greenvehicles/electric-vehicle-myths.

Garza, Alejandro de la. "How Elon Musk Built His Fortune—and Became the Richest Private Citizen in the World." *Time.* December 13, 2021. https://time.com/6127754/elon-musk-net-worth-person-of-the-year.

Higgins, Tim. *Power Play: Tesla, Elon Musk, and the Bet of the Century.* New York: Doubleday, 2021.

McFadden, Christopher. "The Short but Fascinating History of Tesla Electric Cars, Solar, and Clean Energy." Interesting Engineering. April 17, 2023. https://interestingengineering.com/transportation/the-short-but-fascinating-history-of-tesla.

McKenzie, Hamish. *Insane Mode: How Elon Musk's Tesla Sparked an Electric Revolution to End the Age of Oil.* New York: Dutton, 2018.

Rapier, Graham. "Tesla Gigafactories: A Look at the Manufacturing Hubs and Their Future." *Insider.* July 13, 2023. https://www.businessinsider.com/tesla-gigafactory.

Glossary

artificial intelligence the ability of computer systems to perform tasks that normally require human intelligence, such as speech recognition and decision-making

bankruptcy the state of owing more debt than can be paid

board of directors an executive committee that governs the actions of a business or organization

carbon footprint the amount of greenhouse gases that are created by the actions of a person or entity

entrepreneurial related to a person who organizes a new business venture and assumes the risks associated with it

executive a decision-making leader of a company, such as a president or chief executive officer (CEO)

fraud purposely tricking someone to achieve a gain, usually money

greenhouse gas a type of gas in the atmosphere that traps heat, such as carbon dioxide and methane

hybrid composed of two different things

initial public offering
the process of offering shares in a company to the public for the first time

innovation something that is original or advanced beyond the usual

invest to commit money or other resources in order to earn a financial return

lawsuit a claim of wrongdoing brought to a court of law

profit the amount of money that a business keeps after subtracting expenses from revenues

prototype an early model of something from which others are developed or copied

revenue the money earned by a company; another word for income

share an equal interest or right into which the entire stock of a corporation is divided

stock shared ownership in a company by many people who buy shares, or portions, of stock, hoping the company will make a profit and the stock value will increase

Websites

Tesla: About Us

https://www.tesla.com/about
Learn about Tesla's current and future goals.

Tesla, Inc.

www.britannica.com/topic/Tesla-Motors
Read more about Tesla and founder Elon Musk.

Where Is Roadster?

www.whereisroadster.com
Track the location of Starman in real time.

Index